[Issued with Army Orders for August, 1924

T0326021

THE IMPRESSMENT OF HORSES AND HORSE-DRAWN VEHICLES IN TIME OF NATIONAL EMERGENCY

N.B. – In accordance with Section 187 of the Army Act, these instructions do not extend to the Channel Islands and the Isle of Man.

AN EXPLANATION OF THE SYSTEM ADOPTED AND THE LAW AND PROCEDURE IN REGARD THERETO

With detailed instructions for purchasers and those appointed to assist them.

FIRESTEP
Editions

www.firesteppublishing.com

FIRESTEP
Editions

FireStep Publishing
Gemini House
136-140 Old Shoreham Road
Brighton
BN3 7BD

www.firesteppublishing.com

First published by the General Staff, War Office 1924.
First published in this format by FireStep Editions,
an imprint of FireStep Publishing, in association with
the National Army Museum, 2013.

NATIONAL
ARMY
MUSEUM

www.nam.ac.uk

ISBN 978-1-908487-73-5

Cover design FireStep Publishing
Typeset by FireStep Publishing
Printed and bound in Great Britain

Please note: *In producing in facsimile from original historical documents, any
imperfections may be reproduced and the quality may be lower than modern
typesetting or cartographic standards.*

[Issued with Army Orders for August, 1924.

THE IMPRESSMENT OF HORSES AND HORSE–DRAWN VEHICLES IN TIME OF NATIONAL EMERGENCY.

N.B.—*In accordance with Section* 187 *of the Army Act, these instructions do not extend to the Channel Islands and the Isle of Man.*

AN EXPLANATION OF THE SYSTEM ADOPTED AND THE LAW AND PROCEDURE IN REGARD THERETO

With detailed instructions for Purchasers and those appointed to assist them.

Copy issued to .... who has

been appointed to the .... purchasing area

.... Command,

on mobilization for .... years.

These instructions, which should be studied in peace time, come into effect on receipt of orders from the General Officer Commanding-in-Chief the command concerned after mobilization or partial mobilization has been ordered.

It may be necessary to supplement them by instructions and information peculiar to local conditions.

.... Signature of Staff Officer of Command who issues these instructions to a purchaser or distributor,* and whose signature hereto constitutes the gentleman in question a purchaser or a distributor.*

The Memorandum will be issued to—
- (a) Military officers connected with classification and impress-ment.
- (b) Gentlemen who have undertaken the duty of purchasers or distributors on mobilization.
- (c) Any magistrates, police officers, or members of County Associations who may apply to General Officers Commanding-in-Chief for information.

    * Strike out whichever is not applicable.

CONTENTS

———

	PAGE
Definitions and Duties of Officials	3
General Explanation	4
Remount Organization and Arrangements to be made in Peace	5
Procedure for Impressment in Time of War...	8
Detailed Duties of Purchasers	10
Remuneration and Terms of Appointment	11
Payment for Impressed Horses or Vehicles	12
Other Payments	13
Extracts from the Army Act...	16
Forms, Requisitions, Warrants, Notices	20

———————

By Command of the Army Council,

H J Creedy

THE WAR OFFICE,
    30*th May*, 1924.

THE IMPRESSMENT OF HORSES AND HORSE–DRAWN VEHICLES IN TIME OF NATIONAL EMERGENCY.

DEFINITIONS AND DUTIES OF OFFICIALS.

1. A District Remount Officer on mobilization will, under the D.A.D.R., act as a representative of Command Headquarters within his District, and will be ready to give any assistance which Purchasers may require in carrying out the instructions issued by Command Headquarters. The D.R.O. will be responsible for the collection of any boarded-out horses in his district.

A Purchaser is the officer, retired officer or private gentleman appointed to purchase horses (and vehicles if required) on mobilization, in accordance with instructions from Command Headquarters.

A Purchaser is responsible for all arrangements in his area and supervises the working of the Distributors and Collectors.

A Distributor is the officer or retired officer in charge of a collecting centre. He will be responsible for the distribution of the horses bought by the Purchaser to the units requiring them, in accordance with instructions issued by Command Headquarters.

A Collector is a retired officer or private gentleman appointed to assist a Purchaser in collecting horses for purchase, and in all duties except the actual purchase. A Collector may also be appointed to assist the Distributor in his duties, except in the actual allotment of horses to units.

A Collecting Area.—The area from which horses are brought to an appointed collecting centre.

A Collecting Centre.—A centre to which impressed horses are brought for issue to units on mobilization. Boarded-out horses will also be collected at a collecting centre.

A Purchasing Post is a place to which horses may be taken by owners for purchase, when it is not convenient for them to be taken to a collecting centre before purchase. An owner's stable may be a Purchasing Post.

A Place of Collection is the description of the actual stable or field at a collecting centre, at which conducting parties should report for horses, and to which Collectors may be instructed to send horses.

An Entraining Station.—The railway station to which horses are sent for despatch after purchase. A Collecting Centre, or the place of collection, is often the same as the entraining station, but railway premises must not be used as either without the concurrence of the railway authorities.

Boarded-out Horses are Government horses, boarded out to approved allottees under specified conditions, and are liable to immediate recall on mobilization.

Classified Horses.—Horses of private persons and firms, which have been classified as suitable and available for impressment for military purposes in accordance with the provisions of Section 115 of the Army Act (as amended by the Army Annual Act of 1921).

A Purchasing Area.—An area presided over by a Purchaser. It may consist of one or more collecting areas.

A Conducting Party.—A party detailed from a military unit to meet and take over horses from Distributors.

A Collecting Party.—A party of soldiers, reservists, pensioners or civilians, detailed by Command Headquarters, to collect horses at Purchasing Posts and to take them to Collecting Centres.

A Collecting Party should not take over any animals until they have been purchased and branded by the Purchaser.

An Imprest Account. — When money is advanced to an individual who normally is not a paymaster, it is known as Imprest money, and the account rendered by that individual showing how the money has been dealt with is an Imprest Account.

NOTE.—The term vehicle, where it appears in the instructions for purchasers, &c., in this appendix refers to a " horse-drawn " vehicle.

GENERAL EXPLANATION.

2. It is the Law, under Section 115 of the Army Act, that, when His Majesty has by Order signified by a Secretary of State declared a National Emergency to exist, and when certain other conditions laid down in the Army Act have been fulfilled, such animals and vehicles as may be required for the use of His Majesty's Forces may be impressed by the Military Authorities.

The power to impress extends to draught and saddle horses and any other animals used for similar purposes, to all classes of vehicles, including motor-cars and other locomotives, and to all boats, barges, and other vessels used for transport on rivers and canals.

The Act provides that impressment is to be made on the requisition of a General or Field Officer commanding troops and on the authority of a Justice's warrant, and is to be carried out by a police constable acting in pursuance of the Justice's warrant. The owners, on demand of the constable, are obliged to furnish the animals, vehicles, etc., required, which are then handed over to the Military Authorities for consignment to the point where they are needed.

The Act further provides that impressed animals, vehicles, etc., shall be hired or bought at the option of the State, at a price to be fixed by the Officer or private person duly authorized by the Army Council for the purpose. The owner, should he be dissatisfied with the price paid, has the right to appeal to the County Court Judge (in Scotland the Sheriff), who is empowered to settle any difference regarding the price. The appeal must, however, be made within three weeks of the date on which the impressment is made. Purchasers should inform intending appellants of this condition.

The Act also permits the prohibition of the sale and purchase of horses to or by any person other than a person appointed by the Army Council to purchase horses, and imposes penalties on all persons who impede the carrying out of the law in these matters. Purchasers appointed by the Army Council will be provided with a distinctive brassard, which will be worn by them while they are carrying out the duties of their appointments.

3. The law, therefore, recognizes that, while the nation as a whole bears the burden of war, individual convenience must on grave occasions give way to the urgent need of the State; but it also provides that on such occasions fair payment shall be made for those animals and vehicles which the State is compelled to impress.

Under modern conditions it is not possible to put off the preparation for war till war is actually imminent. Full and careful preparation in peace is essential. It has, therefore, been found necessary to arrange that horses and vehicles suitable for war shall be duly surveyed in peace time, and entered in a register; also to provide for an organization which will ensure that the required animals and vehicles can be promptly impressed, paid for, collected, and issued to the troops that require them when the necessity arises.

REMOUNT ORGANIZATION AND ARRANGEMENTS TO BE MADE IN PEACE.

4. With the object indicated above, it has been enacted by the amendments to the Army Act (Section 114), passed in the Army (Annual) Act of 1911, that the Army Council may authorize Officers or other persons to enter private stables at all reasonable hours to ascertain and register the number of horses or vehicles suitable for military purposes contained therein. In normal circumstances this duty will be carried out by Officers acting on behalf of the Army Council, and not by the Police Authorities. The Officers engaged in this duty have been instructed that they should not enter private stables without first obtaining the permission of the owner; should permission be refused, the District Remount Officer will call and explain the reason why such information regarding animals and vehicles is immediately necessary, although the likelihood of their being actually required may be remote. It is anticipated that there will be no refusal on the part of owners when once the situation has been explained; in the event, however, of any still persisting in their refusal, Section 114 of the Army Act, as amended, provides that a Justice may, on application from the Officer who has been obstructed, issue a search warrant, directing a constable to accompany the Officer and enter the premises at any hour between 6 a.m. and 9 p.m. to inspect any animals or carriages that may be found therein.

5. The provision of the necessary number of suitable animals on mobilization is a difficult administrative problem the solution of which depends on two separate factors. *First* the existence of the animals, and, *secondly*, the time in which they can be made available.

6. Numerically there are more animals in the country than are likely to be required in any normal mobilization, and steps must be taken in peace to find out which animals are to be selected for impressment.

The steps taken for this purpose are as follows :—

(a) *A Periodical Census.*—This census shows the horse population of the country, but does not differentiate between the fit and unfit animals. The interval between one census and another will depend on any special circumstances which may influence the horse-breeding industry ; normally it will be about five years. Copies of the census returns will be forwarded by the police direct to District Remount Officers.

(b) *Classification of Horses.*—The horses included in the general census are classified according to their fitness for military duty, with the various Arms of the Service. This initial classification of all animals should be completed within the two years following the census. To enable this to be done each Command is divided into a convenient number of Remount Districts of each of which a District Remount Officer (D.R.O.) has charge. The D.R.O. carries out the classification. He visits the stables where horses are kept (he has access to the census returns). Inspects each horse and enters the result in A.B. 389. The animals of railway companies are exempt from classification. The result of the classification is forwarded to the War Office, which is then able to allot to each Command the number of horses which that Command will be called upon to supply on mobilization. This information, showing the days on which the animals are to be supplied, is published annually in the " Remount Statement."

(c) *Annual Allotment of Horses for Impressment.*—Each Command Headquarters distributes the number allotted to it in the " Remount Statement " among Remount Districts. The D.R.O. thereupon re-classifies sufficient animals to ensure that the Purchaser will be able quickly to obtain the necessary number on mobilization. This re-classification must be carried out every year, and the list of animals kept up to date. In allotting horses the D.R.O. will, as far as possible, draw upon the whole of his district, and not confine himself to any particular part of it. He will normally only allot 50 per cent. from any one stable, and will not take the horses of Public Bodies, Railway Companies, or Food Distributing Businesses unless the required number cannot be obtained without doing so. Animals the property of T.A. Associations are not available for allotment for impressment.

7. The second point to be remembered is the time in which the animals can be made available. To ensure the receipt by Units of impressed horses on the days shown in the " Remount Statement," steps must be taken to complete in peace time all arrangements for the collection and distribution of impressed horses.

The steps consist of :—

(a) *Appointment of Officials.*—The Remount District will be divided into Purchasing Areas according to the number of animals which have to be obtained each day. A Purchaser must be appointed for each Area. A Veterinary Surgeon will be required for each Purchaser. One or more collecting Centres will be necessary for each Purchasing Area ; these and the Distributors who will be in charge of them must be selected beforehand. Collectors to assist the Purchasers must be earmarked. The District Remount Officer will submit the names of suitable individuals to Command Headquarters, by whom the appointments will be made. Care must be taken by the D.R.O. in submitting names that the individuals recommended are such as are likely to work together harmoniously and efficiently.

(b) *Transport Arrangements.*—Arrangements will be made for the steady flow of animals from the Collecting Centre to units either by train or road. The completion of all preliminary arrangements will allow Command Headquarters to draw up a Railway Time Table, which must be adhered to in every particular.

(c) *Reserve Horses.*—The reserve horses, viz., boarded-out horses, will be collected at Collecting Centres by the D.R.Os. and distributed by Distributors in the same way as impressed horses.

PROCEDURE FOR IMPRESSMENT IN TIME OF WAR.

The procedure for impressment in time of war is as follows :—

8. The first step is the declaration of an Emergency. This will be effected by an Order of His Majesty signed by a Secretary of State declaring that a State of Emergency exists, and authorizing the issue of "Requisitions of Emergency" by General or Field Officers.

9. The second step is the issue of requisitions of emergency. These will be signed and issued by the General or Field Officers authorized to do so by the Royal Order, and they will require Justices of the Peace to issue impressment warrants for the provision of animals and vehicles for the purposes mentioned in the requisitions.

The General or Field Officer signing the Requisition of Emergency will notify the public in each area by advertisement of a copy of the signed Requisition in the local press, and by causing to be posted notices (A.F. A2002) informing them that for a specified period no persons other than those specially authorized by the Army Council are allowed to buy or sell horses.

10. The third step is the application to a Justice for the issue of an impressment warrant. This application will be made by an Officer of a portion of His Majesty's Forces mentioned in the "Requisition of Emergency,' or by some other duly authorized Officer, who will go to a Justice, taking with him the "Requisition of Emergency" and a written demand, in the schedule to which the Officer will state the animals and vehicles required for the purpose mentioned in the requisition. The production of the "Requisition of Emergency" to the Justice will be conclusive evidence of the Officer's authority. To save time, he will also take with him, ready for the Justice's signature, a warrant to which the schedule of animals and vehicles required will be attached.

11. The fourth step is the issue of the Justice's warrant. The Justice will, on the production to him of the "Requisition of Emergency" and on the demand of the Officer, at once sign the warrant and issue it to the constables of the County or Borough in which he has jurisdiction. Previous arrangements should be made by the Military Authorities with the Chief Constables for the services of the necessary constables to receive and execute the warrants.

12. It will then be the duty of the constable to whom the warrant is given to proceed to execute it. The constable who holds the warrant is the impressing official, and is required by law to execute the warrant by ordering the owners to furnish the animals and vehicles required. The constable, accompanied by the Collector, will proceed to the premises where the required horses and vehicles are to be found, and will serve on the owner a written notice of the horses and vehicles which he is ordered to furnish.

The Military Officer who hands to the constable the Justice's warrant will also hand him the notices, with the particulars of the required animals and vehicles filled in, and the constable will sign the forms and, as he goes round with the Collector, will serve the proper notice on each owner.

In most cases owners will readily send the animals to Collecting Centres for inspection by the Purchaser if asked to do so,* in any case the duty of the constable ends with the serving of the notice. [Under the conditions of Section 115 (3 A) of the Army Act, owners may be compelled to send horses which have already been impressed to selected Collecting Centres, provided that such Centres are within a 10-mile radius of the owners' stables.] When, however, it is desirable to collect horses at a Purchasing Post prior to Impressment, Purchasers are authorized to pay " bringing money " to grooms (see para. 16(b)). In such cases previous arrangements will generally have been made for owners to send their animals to the selected Purchasing Post.

If any difficulty is made by the owner about giving up the animals and vehicles, it will be the duty of the police to see that the order is enforced.

Collecting Parties should not take charge of any animals until they have been purchased and branded by the Purchaser.

The Act provides that any person who refuses or neglects to furnish the animals and vehicles when ordered by the constable, or impedes in any way the execution of the warrant, shall be liable on summary conviction to a fine, and the animals and vehicles may be removed, if necessary, by force ; the constable will, therefore, warn any person refusing to provide the animals and vehicles, or impeding the execution of the warrant, as to the provisions of the Act in this regard, and will assist the Officer in the event of it being necessary for him to take steps to remove the animals and vehicles by force.

13. The fifth step consists in the actual purchase. The Purchaser will at the time of purchase scissor clip each animal under the saddle on the near side according to the class for which it is intended.

---

* Owners cannot be compelled to send animals before impressment (i.e., purchase) to any Purchasing Post or Collecting Centre.

Riding horses will be scissor clipped	R.
Light draught	,,	,,	L.
Heavy	,,	,,	,,	H.
Pack	,,	,,	P.

The Purchaser will also affix a label to each headstall. The label will contain the name of the Purchaser and any special information which may be of assistance in " posting " the animal on its arrival at its destination, *e.g.* " Hunt horse," " Quiet hack."

The Purchaser will arrange for each animal purchased by him to be branded on the near quarter with the special Identification Brand issued to him, which will be kept with the Purchaser's box.

The impressed animals are then handed over to the Distributor at the Collecting Centre, who will brand each horse with the broad arrow low down on the near fore hoof. Where stabling is not provided and animals have to be tied up in close proximity to each other in order to avoid casualties from kicks, it may be necessary to remove hind shoes—especially those with calkins. All vehicles purchased will be branded in a conspicuous place. The Distributor then issues the horses to conducting parties for conveyance to Units in accordance with instructions received from Command Headquarters.

14. The Commander-in-Chief in each Command is responsible for the details of the scheme for his own Command. The procedure outlined above is the normal, but special arrangements will no doubt be necessary in some cases to meet local conditions. Purchasers will adhere to the instructions issued by Command Headquarters.

DETAILED DUTIES OF PURCHASERS.

15. The duties of Purchasers are to take general charge of the collection and purchase of the horses and vehicles in the Area allotted to them.

16. Their duties include :

(*a*) The purchase to the extent authorized in lists supplied to them by Command Headquarters, of such horses and vehicles as appear to them to be fit for the service. Horses must be passed by the veterinary surgeon as workably sound and free from all suspicious symptoms of contagious disease. When a veterinary surgeon is not available at the place of purchase the Purchaser must use his own judgment as to the workable soundness of the horse.

The act of purchase includes fixing the price and actual payment by means of an order on the Command Paymaster.

ı The price of each horse, which should be the fair market price ruling at the time, is fixed by the Purchaser in accordance with definite data furnished by the War Office to each Command from time to time.

(b) The payment when necessary of a suitable gratuity, as defined in para. **12**, as " bringing money " (not to exceed 5s. a horse) to the man who brings the horses to the appointed Collecting Centre or Purchasing Post.

(c) The scissor clipping with the distinguishing letter according to class (see para. **13**), and the branding on the near quarter of each horse purchased by him (a special brand is issued and kept with the Purchaser's box for this purpose).

(d) The affixing of a label to each horse's headstall. The label should show Purchaser's name and have a note on it of any information that will help in the posting of the animal on arrival at its destination, viz., " Hunt horse," " Quiet hack," etc. (see para. **13**).

(e) The arrangements for the branding by the Distributor of a broad arrow low down on the near fore hoof of each animal, and on all vehicles purchased.

REMUNERATION AND TERMS OF APPOINTMENT.

17. The following allowances are payable to the personnel employed in purchase or collection :—

Civilian or Retired Military Purchasers. Normally £3 a day and actual expenses of locomotion (when an officer of any embodied unit, 5s. a day under para. 500, Allowance Regulations, 1924, together with the usual travelling allowances when necessarily absent from headquarters ; the total of these two allowances, however, which are in addition to pay of rank, not to exceed 30s. a day).

Veterinary Surgeon. £2 a day (when not an Officer of the Special Reserve, or of an embodied Territorial Force Unit). Also actual expenses of locomotion, and allowances at the rates and under the conditions prescribed in the following table :

When absent at night for a period not exceeding 14 nights in one place.	After 14 nights in one place, or for the whole period if the Officer knew before starting that his stay in one place must exceed 14 nights.	When absent above 10 hours, both from usual place of duty and from home, but not absent for a night and for the last day of a journey, if one or more complete periods of 24 hours necessary absence are exceeded by 10 hours.'
*15/-	10/-	*5/-

* These rates are subject to the temporary increases prescribed by Army Council Instruction 225 of 1920.

The above rates are maximum rates which, in cases of prolonged detention at one place, will be liable to reduction to a rate sufficient to cover the reasonable extra expense involved.

Any period in excess of 28 nights at one place, when the probable length of the detention is foreseen, will normally be regarded as coming under this rule, and a reduction may be made for the whole period or for the period in excess of 28 nights, according to the circumstances of the case.

Civilian or Retired Military Officers as Distributors or Collectors.	£1 a day and actual expenses of locomotion.
Clerks (if civilians).	7s. 6d. a day and actual expenses of locomotion.
Grooms, horse-keepers, etc.	5s. a day and actual expenses of locomotion.

18. The hiring of motor cars, or the use of privately-owned motor vehicles, when absolutely necessary for journeys on duty, will be governed by such instructions as will be issued to each Purchaser from Command Headquarters at the commencement of purchasing operations.

(N.B.—Command Headquarters will have these instructions drawn up beforehand. They will be based on the Allowance Regulations and A.C.I. 527 of 1919, as amended by A.C.I. 12 of 1923, and will be suitably corrected and kept up to date as may be necessary. They will also include a notification of the current actual rates of Travelling Allowance referred to in the footnote to para. **17.**)

PAYMENT FOR IMPRESSED HORSES OR VEHICLES.

19. The assessed value of a horse or vehicle will be paid to the owner by the Purchaser, by means of a Payment Order on the Command Paymaster ; such order may be passed to a Bank for collection in the same manner as an ordinary cheque. (A book of Payment Order forms is in each " Purchaser's Box.")

20. No receipt need be taken from owners, but the counterfoil of the Payment Order Book must be filled in as a record. These Payment Orders are not to be used for any other purpose than the actual purchase price of horses or vehicles.

21. The Purchaser will post to the Command Paymaster each night A.F. N 1547, compiled to show :—

(a) Expenditure on purchase of horses and vehicles (being a copy of the counterfoils in Payment Order Book, A.B. 390) during the day in question. The Payment Orders must be entered on this form in strict numerical sequence.

(b) The number of horses or vehicles issued during the day in question, and the unit, depot, or military station to which they have been despatched. Issues will be supported by receipts (usually taken on A.B. 394) from the station master, or from the officer or N.C.O. in charge of a conducting party, which takes the horses, &c., from a collecting centre.

(c) The balance of animals or vehicles remaining on hand (*i.e.*, those actually purchased but not issued) at the time of rendering the Return.

No other accounts of the actual purchase and disposal of animals or vehicles need be rendered by the Purchasers. **The daily posting of this statement is most important to ensure prompt settlement of the Payment Orders.**

OTHER PAYMENTS

22. Money required for the purposes set out in para. **23** should be obtained from the Headquarters of the Command by the Purchaser who will have an initial advance of £200 placed to his credit as soon as purchasing operations are ordered.

He will account for all monies so obtained on A.F. N 1531, which he will complete and balance as soon as he has made all his payments. He will remit the unexpended balance to the Command Cashier, at Command Headquarters, and will forward the A.F. N 1531 with the supporting receipts to his Deputy Assistant Director of Remounts at Command Headquarters.

The D.A.D.R., after satisfying himself that the payments to officials are in order, will countersign the account as attesting his approval of their appointments and periods of employment, and will then transmit the accounts, without delay, to the Command Paymaster.

23. Purchasers are authorized to pay from their Imprest Accounts any expenditure necessarily incurred under the following heads.

Such payments should be detailed on A.F. N 1531, and receipts attached for sums over 5*s*.

(*a*) All remuneration (*i.e.*, Pay) due to civilians or retired military officers, as fixed in para. **17**.

(*b*) Actual expenses of locomotion, except such as may fall under para. **24**.

(*c*) Bringing money, clerks, hire of grooms for collecting parties as horse-holders, &c.

(*d*) Purchase of forage at local market rates for use at collecting stations when these are not at military stations.

(*e*) Hire of stabling for horses unavoidably detained.

(*f*) Purchase of rugs, headstalls, or leading ropes when absolutely necessary.

(*g*) Any minor expenditure, *e.g.*, shoeing, necessarily incurred incidental to collection and despatch by road or rail.

24. Travelling allowances and, when authorised, mileage allowance for privately owned motor vehicles will not be paid from Imprest Account, but will be claimed at the close of Purchasing Operations on A.F. O 1771, which will be forwarded to the D.A.D.R., at Command Headquarters, for approval and transmission to the Command Paymaster, for audit and settlement.

25. Officers Commanding Stations, Receiving Depots, or Units, to which horses are sent by rail, must be informed (by telegram) of the hour of despatch by Distributors.

26. The Purchaser, or Distributor acting for him, will telegraph, at 6 p.m. daily, to Command Headquarters the number by classes of horses :—

(*a*) Boarded-out horses called up.

(*b*) Purchased during the day.

(*c*) Despatched giving units and destination.

(*d*) Remaining on hand.

27. No horses should be purchased from a stable where an infectious disease has been discovered. Any such discovery should be reported at once (by telegram or telephone) to Command Headquarters.

28. The following items of stationery, Army Forms, etc., will be kept in the Purchaser's Box, which will be issued to the Purchaser on mobilization :—

(*a*) A.B. 390, cheque book of payment orders on the Command Cashier (*see* para. **39**).

(*b*) A.B. 391, consignment note (railway transport of purchases).

(*c*) Pamphlet : The Impressment of Horses in Time of National Emergency.

(d) A.F. N 1547, Purchaser's Statement of Account (*see* para. **37**).

(e) A.F. O 1771, form of claim for travelling expenses and travelling allowances.

(f) A.F. N 1531, Statement of Miscellaneous Expenditure.

(g) A supply of tie-on labels and stationery.

(h) Book of Telegraph Forms with carbon paper.

(i) Receipt Book A.B. 394 (*see* para. **38**).

(j) Branding irons.

(k) A.F. N 1487. Requisition for Cash (*see* para. **40**).

(l) A.F. P 1940. Postage a/c.

(m) One pair clipping scissors.

(n) Purchaser's brassard.

(o) A " Pass " for each Collector, Distributor, and Veterinary Officer (to be supplied by Command Headquarters).

(p) A.B. 57. Cash receipt book.

29. The following is a general description of the classes of animals suitable for Military Purposes :—

(a) Chargers for Officers of Mounted Arms. Hunter Class, with manners. 15·2 to 16 hands.

(b) Officers' Cobs, for Officers' Dismounted Branches and Pack Artillery. Hunters. Polo ponies, Hacks with manners. 14·2 to 15·1½ hands.

(c) Cavalry Troop Horse. R.1. Hunt servants' horses and other riding horses with some quality. Short-backed with true action. Should not exceed 15·3 hands.

(d) Riding Horses for Arms other than Cavalry. R.2. Similar type as R.1, with less quality ; should not exceed 15·2 hands.

(e) L.Ds. The type of the old bus horse is the ideal, with plenty of " activity." 15·1 to 15·3 ; weight 1,200 to 1,300 lbs.

(f) H.Ds. The Heavy Artillery Horse. Active type of cart horse, as clean legged (free from feather) as possible, with good feet. Should not exceed 16·1 ; weight, 1,500 to 1,600 lbs.

(g) Pack (Cavalry). The same as Cavalry troop horse.

(h) Pack Ponies. 14 to 14·2 hands ; with straight backs and suitable pack action.

(i) Pack Mules. 13·3 to 14·2 hands. Girth under 14 hands not less than 63 inches ; over 14 hands not less than 64 inches. Straight backs, suitable pack action.

(j) In all cases the following are the most essential points—

(i) Equable temperament.
(ii) Good middle piece.
(iii) Good feet.
(iv) Straight and true action.

N.B.—Light grey horses and those of abnormal colours are not suitable for military purposes.

30. The following paragraphs contain the principal provisions of the Army Act relating to impressment; also copies of the requisitions, warrants and notices referred to in the preceding paragraphs, which should be brought by the Military Officers concerned to the Justices and constables prior to carrying out the impressed purchase described. The detailed instructions regarding classification and impressment are laid down in the Remount Regulations.

EXTRACTS FROM THE ARMY ACT.

31. 114.—(1) The authority hereinafter mentioned for any place may cause annually a list to be made out of all persons in such place, or any particular part thereof, liable to furnish carriages and animals under this Act, and of the number and description of the carriages and animals of such persons; and where a list is so made, any justice may by warrant require any constable or constables having authority within such place to give from time to time, on demand by an Officer or Non-Commissioned Officer under this Act, orders to furnish carriages and animals, and such warrant shall be executed as if it were a special warrant issued in pursuance of this Act on such demand, and the orders shall specify the like particulars as such special warrant.

(1A) For the purpose of assisting the authority hereinafter mentioned in the preparation of such list as aforesaid, any proper Officer authorized in that behalf by the Authority shall be entitled at all reasonable times to enter any premises in which he has reason to believe that any carriages or animals are kept, and to inspect any carriages or animals which may be found therein.

In this provision the expression " proper Officer " means any Officer or person of such rank, class or description as may be specified in an order of the Army Council made for the purpose.

(1B) With respect to horses, the following provisions shall have effect—

(a) It shall be the duty of the owner of any horse, and the occupier of any premises where horses are kept, to furnish, if so required, to the Authority hereinafter mentioned, before such date in each year as may be prescribed, a return specifying the number of horses belonging to him or kept on his premises, and giving with respect to every horse such details as may be so prescribed; he shall also afford all reasonable facilities for enabling any horse belonging to him or kept on his premises to be inspected and examined as and when required by the said Authority ; if any person fails to comply with any of the requirements of this paragraph, he shall be liable on summary conviction for each offence to a fine not exceeding fifty pounds ;

(b) The Army Council may, for the purposes of this Sub-section, make regulations prescribing anything which under this Sub-section is to be prescribed, and prescribing the forms to be used, and generally for the purpose of carrying this Sub-section into effect ;

(c) Regulations made by the Army Council may provide for excepting from the provisions of this Sub-section horses of any class or description specified in the regulations.

(2) The Authority hereinafter mentioned shall cause such list to be kept at some convenient place open for inspection at all reasonable times by persons interested, and any person who feels aggrieved either by being entered in such list, or by being entered to furnish any number or description of carriages or animals which he is not liable to furnish, may complain to a Court of Summary Jurisdiction, and the Court, after such notice as the Court think necessary to persons interested, may order the list to be amended in such manner as the Court may think just.

(3) All orders given by constables for furnishing carriages and animals shall, as far as possible, be made from such list in regular rotation.

(3A) If any Officer is obstructed in the exercise of his powers under this Section, a Justice of the Peace may, if satisfied by information on oath that the Officer has been so obstructed, issue a search warrant authorizing the constable named therein, accompanied by the Officer, to enter the premises in respect of which the obstruction took place at any time between six o'clock in the morning and nine o'clock in the evening, and to inspect any carriages or animals that may be found therein.

(4) The Authority for the purposes of this Section shall be the Army Council, or any Authority or persons to whom the Army Council may delegate their powers under this Section.

115.—(1) His Majesty, by order, distinctly stating that a case of emergency exists, and signified by a Secretary of State, * * * * * * * * * * * * * * * * * * may authorize any General or Field Officer Commanding His Majesty's regular forces in any Military District or place in the United Kingdom to issue a requisition under this Section (hereinafter referred to as a Requisition of Emergency).

(2) The Officer so authorized may issue a Requisition of Emergency under his hand reciting the said order, and requiring Justices of the Peace to issue their warrants for the provision, for the purpose mentioned in the Requisition, of such carriages and animals as may be provided under the foregoing provisions, and also of carriages of every description (including motor-cars and other locomotives, whether for the purpose of carriage or haulage), and of horses of every description, whether kept for saddle or draught, and also of vessels (whether boats, barges, or other) used for the transport of any commodities whatsoever upon any canal or navigable river, and also of food, forage, and stores of every description.

(3) A Justice of the Peace, on demand by an Officer of the portion of His Majesty's forces mentioned in a Requisition of Emergency, or by an Officer of the Army Council authorized in this behalf, and on production of the Requisition, shall issue his warrant for the provision of such carriages, animals, vessels, food, forage, and stores as are stated by the Officer producing the Requisition of Emergency to be required for the purpose mentioned in the Requisition ; the warrant shall be executed in the like manner, and all the provisions of this Act as to the provision or furnishing of carriages and animals, including those respecting fines on Officers, Non-Commissioned Officers, Justices, constables, or owners of carriages or animals, shall apply in like manner as in the case where a Justice issues, in pursuance of the foregoing provisions of this Act, a warrant for the provision of carriages and animals, and shall apply to vessels, food, forage and stores, in like manner in all respects as they apply to carriages.

(3A) A Requisition of Emergency may authorize any Officer mentioned therein to require any carriages and horses furnished in pursuance of this Section to be delivered at such place (not being more than one hundred miles in the case of a motor-car or other locomotive, and not being more than ten miles in the case of any other carriage or horse, from the premises of the owner), and at such time as may be specified by any officer mentioned in the Requisition, and in such case it shall be the duty of a constable executing a warrant issued by a Justice of the Peace under this Section upon the demand of an Officer producing the Requisition of Emergency to insert in his order such time and place for delivery of any vehicle or horse to which the order relates as may be specified by such Officer, and the obligation of owners to furnish carriages and horses shall include an obligation to deliver the carriages and horses at such place and time as may be specified in such order, and the provisions of this Act shall have effect as if references therein to the furnishing of carriages and horses included, as respects any such carriage or horse as aforesaid, delivery at such time and place as aforesaid.

(4) The Army Council shall cause due payment to be made for articles furnished in pursuance of this section, and if any difference

arises respecting the amount of payment for any article, the amount shall be such as may be fixed by a certificate of a County Court Judge having jurisdiction in any place in which such article was furnished or through which it travelled or was carried in pursuance of the requisition ; and for the purpose of fixing such amount the provisions set out in the Sixth Schedule to this Act shall have effect.

Where a sum has been paid or tendered by or on behalf of the Army Council under this Sub-section, that sum shall be deemed to be the amount due, unless within three weeks from the date of payment or tender, an application is made to a County Court Judge for his certificate.

(5) Canal, river or lock tolls are hereby declared not to be demandable for vessels while employed in any service in pursuance of this Section or returning therefrom. And any toll collector who demands or receives toll in contravention of this exemption shall, on summary conviction, be liable to a fine not exceeding £5 nor less than 10s.

(6) A Requisition of Emergency, purported to be issued in pursuance of this Section and to be signed by an Officer therein stated to be authorized in accordance with this Section, shall be evidence, until the contrary is proved, of its being duly issued and signed in pursuance of this Act, and if delivered to an Officer of His Majesty's forces or of the Army Council shall be a sufficient authority to such Officer to demand carriages, animals, vessels, food, forage, and stores in pursuance of this Section, and when produced by such Officer shall be conclusive evidence to a Justice and constable of the authority of such Officer to make such demand in accordance with such requisition ; and it shall be lawful to convey on such carriages, animals, and vessels, not only the baggage, provisions, and military stores of the troops mentioned in the Requisition of Emergency, but also the Officers, soldiers, servants, women, children, and other persons of and belonging to the same.

(7) Whenever a proclamation ordering the Army Reserve to be called out on permanent service is in force, the order of His Majesty authorizing an Officer to issue a Requisition of Emergency may authorize him to extend such Requisition to the provision of carriages, animals, vessels, food, forage, and stores for the purpose of being purchased, as well as of being hired, on behalf of the Crown.

(8) Where a Justice, on demand by an Officer and on production of a Requisition of Emergency, has issued his warrant for the provision of any articles, and any person ordered in pursuance of such warrant to furnish any such article refuses or neglects to furnish the same according to the order, then, if a proclamation ordering the Army Reserve to be called out on permanent service is in force, the said Officer may seize (and if need be by force) the article requisitioned, and may use the same in like manner as if it had been furnished in pursuance of the order, but the said person

shall be entitled to payment for the same in like manner as if he had duly furnished the same according to the order.

(9) The Army Council may, by regulations under the Territorial and Reserve Forces Act, 1907, assign to County Associations established under that Act the duty of furnishing in accordance with the directions of the Army Council, such carriages, animals, vessels, food, forage, and stores as may be required on mobilization for the regular or auxiliary forces, or any part thereof, and where such regulations are made an officer of a County Association shall have the same powers as are by this Section conferred on an Officer of the Army Council.

(10) A Requisition of Emergency issued under this Section may prohibit, during such period as may be specified in the Requisition, the sale and purchase of horses to or by any persons other than a person appointed by the Army Council to purchase horses ; and if any person sells or purchases or is concerned in the sale or purchase of a horse in contravention of such prohibition, he shall be liable on summary conviction to a fine not exceeding £100, or to imprisonment for a term not exceeding three months, or to both such imprisonment and fine.

190.—(40) The expression " horse " includes a mule, and the provisions of this Act shall apply to any beast of whatever description used for burden or draught or for carrying persons in like manner as if such beast were included in the expression " horse."

SPECIMEN ARMY FORMS AND SHEETS OF ARMY BOOKS.

Army Form A 2029.

32. HORSE, VEHICLE, FOOD, FORAGE, AND STORES IMPRESSMENT.

Containing—

A.—Requisition of Emergency.

A.A.—Notice of Prohibition of Sale or Purchase of Horses.

B.—Demand on Justices by the Officer collecting horses, vehicles, food, forage, and stores.

C.—Justice's Warrant to the Constables to impress.

D.—Constable's notice to owners (100 copies).

NOTE.—Form A above is in itself sufficient to cover any convenient number of B, C, D, while Forms B and C cover any number of D. These books are bound up with one copy of A and A.A., 4 copies of B and C, and 100 of D, merely to provide a useful collection of Forms. Forms A, or Forms A, AA, B and C, may be torn out, to make the books suit the particular case.

(A.)

REQUISITION OF EMERGENCY.

(Army Form A 2029).

(A.)

**Requisition of Emergency (under the Army Act, Section 115)
for the provision of Carriages, Animals and Vessels, and
also of Food, Forage and Stores of every description for
use of His Majesty's Forces.**

*Requisition
to be filled in
and signed
by General
Field
Officer au-
orized to
issue it, or
under S. 171
the Army
ct by a
staff Officer
who is au-
orized to
act on behalf
of those
officers, and
shall be ex-
essed as
signing on
their behalf.*

*After signa-
ture this re-
quisition is
to be for-
warded di-
rect to "Pur-
chasers."*

Whereas His Majesty, in pursuance of Section 115 of the Army Act, has by order dated ....

and signified by ....

a Secretary of State, been pleased to order and authorize any General or Field Officer Commanding His Majesty's Regular Forces in any military district or place in Great Britain and Northern Ireland to issue a requisition of emergency under the said section for the provision for the purposes mentioned in the requisition of such carriages, animals and vessels as are mentioned in the said section, and also of food, forage and stores of every description, and to order and authorize any such officer to extend such requisition to the provision of carriages, animals, vessels, food, forage and stores for the purpose of being purchased, as well as being hired, on behalf of the Crown.

Now, therefore, I, ... being a General (Field) Officer Commanding His Majesty's Regular Forces in .... do hereby issue a Requisition of Emergency in pursuance of the said Order and do hereby require Justices of the Peace to issue their warrants for the provision of such carriages, animals, vessels, food, forage and stores as aforesaid as the same may be demanded by authorized officers for the use of His Majesty's forces in a fit state for such purpose.

And I further authorize .... to require that the carriages and horses furnished under such warrant shall be delivered at such place (not being more than 100 miles in the case of a motor car or other locomotive and not being more than 10 miles in the case of any other carriage or horse, from the premises of the owner) and at such times as may be specified by the said ....

And I hereby prohibit during the period of ...... days, beginning at the date of this requisition, the sale or purchase of horses in the County of ....* within the Petty Sessional Division of .... (or Borough of ....) to or by any person other than a person appointed by the Army Council (or the Air Council) to purchase horses.

To the Justices of the ....

Place ....

Signature ....

Date ....

(A.A.)

NOTICE OF PROHIBITION OF SALE OR PURCHASE OF HORSES.

Take notice that under a requisition of emergency issued by me to the justices of .... on the .... day of .... 19 ......, in accordance with the powers duly conferred on me by order of His Majesty under the Army Act, the sale or purchase of horses in the County of ....* within the Petty Sessional Division of .... (or Borough of ....) to or by any person other than a person appointed by the Army Council [or the Air Council] to purchase horses is prohibited during the period of .... days, beginning at the said date.

Signature ....

General (Field) Officer Commanding His

Majesty's Regular Forces in ....

Note.—This notice requires to be made public. This should be done by advertisement in the local press, and by poster (A.F. A 2002).

* In Scotland these words must be struck out, and in Northern Ireland the words " Petty Sessions District of " must be substituted.

(B.)

DEMAND ON THE JUSTICE BY THE OFFICER COLLECTING HORSES, VEHICLES, FOOD, FORAGE, STORES, OF EVERY DESCRIPTION.

Demand to Justice for Issue of Warrant (under the Army Act, S. 115) for the provision of Carriages, Animals, and Vessels, and also of Food, Forage and Stores of every description for use of His Majesty's Forces.

emand 2 be filled ndsigned Officer oducing above resition of ergency.

In pursuance of Section 115 of the Army Act and the Requisition of Emergency which I produce, I, ...
being an Officer of His Majesty's Regular Forces in ....
....
(being an Officer of His Majesty's Forces at ....,
(being an Officer of the Army Council duly authorized in this behalf),
(being an Officer of the County Association of ....
duly authorized in this behalf), hereby require you to issue your
warrant for the provision within .... days (hours)
of the carriages, animals, vessels, food, forage, and stores mentioned
in the attached schedule* to be delivered at the places and times
mentioned therein, which are required for the use of His Majesty's
Forces in a fit state for such purpose.

To ....

Signature ....

Justice of the Peace for ....

Place ....

Date ....

* Usually on Army Form A 2034 (Outer Sheet).

(C.)

THE JUSTICE'S WARRANT.

Warrant under S. 115 of the Army Act for the provision of Carriages, Animals, Vessels, and also of Food, Forage, and Stores of every description for use of His Majesty's Forces.

In the County of .... *Petty Sessional Division of .... (or Borough of ....).

To each and all of the constables of ....

A demand has been made in pursuance of a Requisition of Emergency produced to me by.., being an Officer of the portion of His Majesty's Forces mentioned in the said Requisition of Emergency (being an Officer of the Army Council duly authorized in that behalf) (being an Officer of the County Association of .... duly authorized in that behalf) for the provision, for use of His Majesty's Forces, of the carriages,† animals,† vessels, food, forage, and stores mentioned in the Schedule attached to this warrant.

You are therefore hereby commanded, on demand being made to you for the purpose by the said ...., to order the several persons in whose possession or control any such carriages, animals, vessels, food, forage, and stores may be, to furnish the same in a fit state for use for the said purpose, at such times and such places as are set out in the said schedule.

Dated the...........................day of .... 19 .

Justice of the Peace for the County (or Borough)
aforesaid (L. S.)

* In Scotland these words must be struck out, and in Northern Ireland the words " Petty Sessions District of " must be substituted.

† Include harness and stable gear if required.

(D.)

NOTICE TO BE SIGNED BY THE CONSTABLE AND HANDED TO THE OWNERS.

G.   R.

NATIONAL EMERGENCY. IMPRESSMENT ORDER UNDER SECTION 115 OF THE ARMY ACT.

ouuterfoil.

To ....

Impress-ment order.

His Majesty having declared that a national emergency has arisen (*and the Army Reserve having been called out on permanent service), the horses, vehicles, vessels, food, forage and stores enumerated below are, if found suitable, to be impressed for hire (or purchase*) in accordance with Section 115 of the Army Act, and to be furnished by you in a state fit for the use of His Majesty's Forces, to be delivered at the time and places set out below. The Army Council will cause due payment to be made for articles furnished as above, and should you not accept the amount paid or tendered as fair value, you have the right to appeal to the County Court (in Scotland the Sheriff's Court) within three

Horses, vehicles, food, forage and stores impressed.

weeks from the date of payment or tender, but you must not hinder the provision of the articles requisitioned. The purchasing officer may claim for hire (*or purchase) such harness and stable gear as he may require with a horse or vehicle, or such fuel, lubricants, illuminants and accessories as he may require with any motor vehicle.

				Place of delivery.	Date and time of delivery.
Horses	...	...	...		
Vehicles	...	...	...		
Vessels	...	...	...		
Food ...	...	...	...		
Forage...	...	...	...		
Stores ...	...	...	...		

* To be omitted if the Army Reserve has not been called out on permanent service.

SECRET.

Army Form A 8.

33. PURCHASER'S SUMMARY.

List of Animals, by Classes, to be purchased in

No...........Purchasing Area.............Command, during Mobilization.

Purchaser's Name .... Address ....

Purchasers will buy the animals shown on this list and arrange for them to arrive at the Collecting Centre on the days of Mobilization mentioned.

Your attention is called to the note on A.F. A 10.

Available Animals, including a percentage of spare, are shown on A.F. A 10.

Day of Mobilization on which Animals should arrive at Collecting Centre.	Collecting Centre to which Horses are to be sent.		Number to be purchased.								
	Place of Collection.	Collecting Centre.	Chargers.	Cobs.	R.1.	R.2.	L.D.	H.D.	Pack.	Mules.	Total.
		Total ...									

.... (Signature).

Command

Army Form A 6.

SECRET.

34. DISTRIBUTOR'S SUMMARY.

Summary of Horses to be despatched from Collecting Centre at ....

No..............Purchasing Area ....Command, during Mobilization.

The details, including train arrangements for each Unit, are shown on Army Forms A 7 attached.

This form will be compiled by Command Headquarters and issued to the Purchaser for the use of Distributors.

Ref. No.	Day of Mobilization on which Animals are to be despatched.	Unit.	Place to which Animals will be sent.	How to be sent by road or rail, etc.	Whether Conducting Party will be sent by Unit.	Number to be despatched.									Remarks.
						Chargers.	Cobs.	R.1.	R.2.	L.D.	H.D.	Pack.	Mules.	Total.	
					Total ...										

Army Form A 10.

SECRET.

35. HORSES ALLOTTED FOR IMPRESSMENT.

List of Horses allotted for Impressment, in   No.......... ....……..Purchasing Area.

Purchaser ……………   ……...............……………………Command.

Collecting Centre to which horses will be sent …………………… ……

The horses shown below have been classified as suitable and allotted for impressment.

The actual number to be purchased is shown on A.F. A "8."

NOTE.—Not more than 50 per cent. of horses owned are to be impressed from any one owner, except in case of single horses. The numbers given below should not be exceeded from any individual stable.

A copy of this form will be required for each Collecting Centre and should be attached to A.F. A 8.

Name and occupation of owner.	Address of		Number of horses kept.		Number which may be impressed.								
	Owner.	Stables where it differs from that of owner.	Property of owner.	Boarded out.	Chargers.	Cobs.	R.1.	R.2.	L.D.	H.D.	Pack.	Mules.	Total.
			Total										

SECRET.

Army Form A 7.

36. ANIMAL REQUIREMENTS OF INDIVIDUAL UNITS ON MOBILIZATION.

(a) Reference Number to correspond with that entered in Col. 1 of A.F. A 6....................

(b) Unit ....

(c) Stationed at ....

....

(d) Telegraphic Address of Unit ....

....

(e) Number of animals to be sent to Unit.

Chargers.	Cobs.	R.1.	R.2.	L.D.	H.D.	Pack.	Mules.	Total.

(f) Animals will be supplied from No. .... Purchasing Area. Collecting Centre will be at ....

(g) A Conducting Party from Unit will take over the horses at (place of collection)...

.... at (hour) .... on

.... day of mobilization.

(h) The Conducting Party to reach Collecting Centre will leave (railway station)...................................

at (hour) .... on ....

day of Mobilization, arriving at (station) ....

at (hour) .... on ....

day of Mobilization, and will report to representative of the Distributor (name) ....

at the place of collection, *see* (g).

(*i*) Horses will be despatched to Unit from (entraining station)
.... at (hour) ....
on .... day of Mobilization, arriving at
destination .... at (hour) ....
on .... day of Mobilization.

(*j*) Number of trucks required ....

(*k*) The railway time tables shown on this form have
been arranged with railway companies concerned.
Distributors should keep in touch with Station Masters
concerned in order to ensure that the trucks are duly
provided. In case of special difficulty application
should be made to

....

whose telegraphic address is ....

....

This form will be compiled by Command Headquarters. The
items which are not applicable will be struck out. One copy will
be issued to the Unit, and one will be attached to the Distributors
Summary, A.F. A 6, and issued to the Purchaser for the use of
the Distributor.

Army Form N 1547.

37. PURCHASE OF HORSES OR VEHICLES ON MOBILIZATION.

Daily Account.

To be rendered to the Command Paymaster at the close of each day's business.

PURCHASES.

			Detail of Payment Orders issued this day.			
Serial No. of payment Order.*	Name of Payee.	Total of each order. £ s. d.	Numbers purchased.†			For use of the Command Paymaster.
			Horses.	Vehicles.		
				Motor.	Other.	
	Balance of yesterday's account.					
	Daily totals ...					

* The continuity of the Sequence Numbers to be strictly maintained.

† A statement in manuscript is to be attached to this form when rendered daily giving a description of each horse bought and the actual price paid for it. This description need not be in great detail, it will be sufficient to state colour, sex, age, height and classification. In making out this statement Purchasers will be careful to enter up animals in the exact sequence in which they were bought.

ISSUES TO DEPOTS, UNITS, &c.

N.B. Receipts (Army Book 394) must be obtained from Station-masters or N.C.Os. i/c Convoys for all horses or vehicles despatched, and should be attached in support of this Table.

Destination (Military Station, Unit, Horse, Depot, &c.).	Number despatched.			Method of despatch (e.g., 'Rail' or 'Convoy').	No. of receipt (attached).
	Horses.	Vehicles.			
		Motor.	Other.		
Totals of this day's issues ...					
Balance remaining on hand				To be carried forward to next day's account	

CERTIFIED that the foregoing is an accurate record of to-day's transactions, and that the balance correctly represents the numbers of Animals and Vehicles purchased but not yet disposed of.

.... Purchaser.

.... Date. .... Area.

38. ARMY BOOK 394.

Purchasers should obtain a receipt for all horses and vehicles, which they have purchased, on this form from the Officer, N.C.O., or soldier in charge of a conducting party or Unit to whom they hand the said horses and vehicles, or if the horses are despatched by train from the Railway Official who receives them for consignment.

Army Book 394.

Army Book 394.

Receipt for Horses forwarded to
Units, etc. .

(Town) .... (Date) .... 19 .

(Date).....................

RECEIPT

Received from* ....

From .... †Horses, for consignment to

....

for...............†Horses   ....

....

sent to

....(Name).

.........................(Station)

* Insert name of Purchaser.   † When necessary add vehicle.

---

39. ARMY BOOK 390.

Horse and Vehicle Impressment.

ORDER FOR PAYMENT.

INSTRUCTIONS.

1. The Purchaser to whom this Book is issued will be careful to keep it under lock and key.

2. He will be responsible that no form is improperly used or extracted from it.

3. Upon handing over at close of operations he should take a receipt.

4. Payment Orders should be made out entirely by the Purchaser and not by a clerk or other person.

5. *It is essential that every payment order should be DATED at the time of signature.*

This Order must be presented within two months, but not earlier than three days, after the date thereof. It may, however, be paid in at once to a bank for collection from the Command Paymaster.

EMERGENCY PAYMENT—HORSE AND VEHICLE IMPRESSMENT.

No. 000001.   Date ....

To the COMMAND PAYMASTER (Eastern, Southern, &c.) Command.
                    (London, Salisbury, &c.)

    Pay to .... (*Name*).

               .... (*Full address*).

The sum of (*in words*) ....

on	...........horses for £	
account	...........vehicles and harness for £	
of	...........motor vehicles for £	

£   :   : .

                  .... Purchaser.

                  .... Purchasing Area.

Received the above sum

> Receipt
> Stamp
> for £2 &
> upwards.

....*Signature.*

                  ....*Date.*

NOTE.—The attention of the Vendor is drawn to the Instructions printed on the back of this Payment Order.

INSTRUCTIONS TO VENDOR.

1. This document should preferably be taken to a local bank for collection. If it is impracticable to collect through a bank it may be forwarded to the Command Paymaster direct.

2. No duplicate of this document can be issued and no responsibility can be assumed by the War Department in the event of its being lost, or of its being cashed fraudulently by another person.

40. REQUISITION FOR CASH.

Army Form N 1487.

(Not to be rendered in duplicate.)

.... { Regiment or Corps. } ....

Station..........

Date..........19..........

CASH required for the period ending ....

Company, etc.	Company, etc., Officer. (Name, Initials, and Rank.)	Station.	Dates on which money is required.	Issue to be made by separate cheque to each Company, etc., Officer. £	Issue to be made by one cheque to the Adjutant or Quartermaster. £	Issue to be made in Cash.† £
			Total ...			

£   s.   d.

† Cash required :—Notes { £1 ... ... 10s. ... ... } Silver in £5 bags

The Account will be rendered to the Paymaster* ....

The Cashier ....

Station..........

Date..........19..........

{ Adjutant, Quarter-master, or Officer Commanding Company, etc. }

* To be filled in by the Officer making the demand.

(B 28/325)Q   Wt 1473-26/Ptg/1073   10M   8/24   H & S Ltd.   Gp. 28.

THE IMPRESSMENT OF HORSES AND HORSE-DRAWN VEHICLES IN TIME OF NATIONAL EMERGENCY

AMENDMENTS NO. 1

N.B. – In accordance with Section 187 of the Army Act, these instructions do not extend to the Channel Islands and the Isle of Man.

AN EXPLANATION OF THE SYSTEM ADOPTED AND THE LAW AND PROCEDURE IN REGARD THERETO

With detailed instructions for purchasers and those appointed to assist them.

FIRESTEP
Editions

www.firesteppublishing.com

The Impressment of Horses and Horse-drawn Vehicles in Time of National Emergency, 1924

AMENDMENTS No. 1

The following amendments will be made to the pamphlet issued with Army Order 335 of 1924 :—

26
Regula-
tions
554

1. Page 11. Paragraph 17 (as amended by Army Order 37 of 1925). *Delete* from line 3 to end of page and corresponding footnote, and *substitute*—

Amdt. 1.
Mar., 1928.

" *Purchasing officers and veterinary surgeons.*

Normally at the rate of £500 a year with the addition of cost of living bonus, and actual expenses of locomotion. If casually employed for a short period only, or for odd days, the rate of emolument will be up to a maximum of £3 a day for each day of employment, with actual expenses of locomotion, but this daily rate will not be issued for more than an aggregate of 28 days, after which pay for further periods of employment will be at the annual rate named above. Officers of the Regular Army Reserve of Officers, *the Militia,* the Supplementary Reserve, the Territorial Army and the Territorial Army Reserve employed as purchasing officers or veterinary surgeons will serve as such only in a civilian capacity at the foregoing rates. They will be ineligible for any benefits granted by the Pay Warrant, 1926, to which they would have been eligible if employed in a military capacity.

2. Page 12, paragraph 17—

Delete table and footnote thereto.

Line 20—

Before " £1 " *insert* an asterisk.

Line 24—

Before " 7*s.* 6*d.*" *insert* an asterisk.

Line 26—

Before " 5*s.*" *insert* an asterisk.

Insert footnote.

Amdt. 1.
Mar.. 1928.
* These figures are only to be taken as a guide, on mobilisation prevailing conditions will be observed in fixing suitable rates of remuneration.

3. Page 14, paragraph 23. *For* sub-paragraph (*d*) *substitute*—

Amdt. 1.
Mar.. 1928.
" (*d*) Purchase of forage at local market rates for use at collecting stations when it is not practicable to obtain it from military stations."

4. Page 18, paragraph (2). *Delete* from "(including" in line 6 to "haulage)" in line 7.

5. Page 18, paragraph (3A).
Line 15. *After* " order," *insert*—

Amdt. 1.
Mar.. 1928.
" notwithstanding that a receipt may be given by the officer mentioned in the warrant at the time of impressment ".

Add at end—

Amdt. 1.
Mar.. 1928.
" The carriages or horses mentioned in the order shall not be deemed to have been furnished until proper delivery has been made to the place and at the time stated in the order."

6. Pages 18 and 19. *For* paragraph (4) *substitute*—

Amdt. 1.
Mar.. 1928.
" (4) The sum to be paid for any article shall be deemed to have been tendered when a formal receipt for the article, setting forth the amount, is handed to the owner or his representative, but the property in a carriage or animal impressed shall be vested in the owner until such time as the carriage or animal has been duly furnished at the place and time stipulated."

3

7. Page 20, paragraph (10).

Line 3—
   After " horses " *insert* " or carriages ".

Line 5—
   After " horses " *insert* " or carriages ".

Line 6—
   After " horse " *insert* " or carriage ".

By Command of the Army Council,

THE WAR OFFICE,
   31*st March*, 1928

THE IMPRESSMENT OF HORSES AND HORSE-DRAWN VEHICLES IN TIME OF NATIONAL EMERGENCY

AMENDMENTS NO. 2

N.B. – In accordance with Section 187 of the Army Act, these instructions do not extend to the Channel Islands and the Isle of Man.

AN EXPLANATION OF THE SYSTEM ADOPTED AND THE LAW AND PROCEDURE IN REGARD THERETO

With detailed instructions for purchasers and those appointed to assist them.

FIRESTEP
Editions

www.firesteppublishing.com

[Crown copyright reserved

[Notified in Army Orders for July, 1929

The Impressment of Horses and Horse-drawn Vehicles in Time of National Emergency, 1924

AMENDMENTS No. 2

The following amendment will be made to the pamphlet notified in Army Order 335 of 1924 :—

Page 12.   *Delete* last two lines of "(N.B. . . .)" to paragraph 18.

26 ─────
Regula-
tions
─────
554

By Command of the Army Council,

THE WAR OFFICE,
    31*st July*, 1929

57—9999

THE IMPRESSMENT OF HORSES AND HORSE-DRAWN VEHICLES IN TIME OF NATIONAL EMERGENCY
AMENDMENTS NO. 3

N.B. – In accordance with Section 187 of the Army Act, these instructions do not extend to the Channel Islands and the Isle of Man.

AN EXPLANATION OF THE SYSTEM ADOPTED AND THE LAW AND PROCEDURE IN REGARD THERETO

With detailed instructions for purchasers and those appointed to assist them.

FireStep
Editions

www.firesteppublishing.com

THE IMPRESSMENT OF HORSES AND HORSE-DRAWN VEHICLES IN TIME OF NATIONAL EMERGENCY, 1924

AMENDMENTS No. 3

Extracts from the Army Act.

1. *For* Section 114 (pages 16 and 17) *substitute—*

114.—(1) The provisions of this subsection shall have effect with respect to horses and mechanically propelled carriages and trailers :—

(*a*) It shall be the duty of the owner of any horse, and the occupier of any premises where horses are kept, to furnish, if so required, to the authority hereinafter mentioned before such date in each year as may be prescribed a return specifying the number of horses belonging to him or kept on his premises, and giving with respect to every horse such details as may be so prescribed ; he shall also afford all reasonable facilities for enabling any horse belonging to him or kept on his premises to be inspected and examined as and when required by the said authority ; if any person fails to comply with any of the requirements of this paragraph, he shall be liable on summary conviction for each offence to a fine not exceeding fifty pounds. The Army Council may, for the purposes of this paragraph, make regulations prescribing anything which under this paragraph is to be prescribed, and prescribing the forms to be used, and generally for the purpose of carrying this paragraph into effect, and the regulations so made may provide for excepting from the provisions of this paragraph horses of any class or description specified in the regulations ;

(*b*) The provisions of the foregoing paragraph shall apply in relation to mechanically propelled carriages and trailers as they apply in relation to horses.

(2) The authority hereinafter mentioned for any place may cause annually a list to be made out of all persons in such place, or any particular part thereof, liable to furnish carriages and animals under this Act, and of the number and description of the carriages and animals of such persons ; and where a list is so made, any justice may by warrant require any constable or constables having authority within such place to give from time to time, on demand by an officer or non-commissioned officer under this Act, orders to furnish carriages and animals, and such warrant shall be executed as if it were a special warrant issued in pursuance of this Act on such demand, and the orders shall specify the like particulars as such special warrant.

(3) The authority hereinafter mentioned shall cause such list to be kept at some convenient place open for inspection at all reasonable times by persons interested, and any person who feels aggrieved either by being entered in such list, or by being entered to furnish any number or description of carriages or animals which he is not liable to furnish, may complain to a court of summary jurisdiction, and the court, after such notice as the court think necessary to persons interested, may order the list to be amended in such manner as the court may think just.

(4) All orders given by constables for furnishing carriages and animals shall, as far as possible, be made from such list in regular rotation.

(5) For the purpose of assisting the authority hereinafter mentioned in the preparation of such list as aforesaid, any proper officer authorised in that behalf by the authority shall be entitled at all reasonable times to enter any premises in which he has reason to believe that any carriages or animals are kept, and to inspect any carriages or animals which may be found therein.
In this provision the expression " proper officer " means any officer or person of such rank, class, or description as may be specified in an order of the Army Council made for the purpose.

(6) If any officer is obstructed in the exercise of his powers under this section, a justice of the peace may, if satisfied by information on oath that the officer has

3

been so obstructed, issue a search warrant authorising the constable named therein, accompanied by the officer, to enter the premises in respect of which the obstruction took place at any time between six o'clock in the morning and nine o'clock in the evening, and to inspect any carriages or animals that may be found therein.

(7) The authority for the purposes of this section shall be the Army Council or any authority or persons to whom the Army Council may delegate their powers under this section.

2. Page 17. Section 115. Sub-section (1). Line 4 from bottom of page. *For* " His Majesty's " *substitute* " the ".

3. Page 18. Section 115. Sub-section (3A).

Lines 4 and 5, *for* " motor-car or other locomotive," *substitute* " mechanically propelled carriage or trailer,".
Line 6, *for* " or horse " *substitute* " or any horse ".

4. Page 19. Section 115. Sub-section (7). *Add* at end—

Amdt. 3
June, 1934

and as respects any mechanically propelled carriage or trailer so requisitioned for the purpose of being purchased, two hundred and fifty miles from the premises of the owner shall for the purposes of subsection (3A) of this section be the distance within which delivery may be required.

110
General
4587

5. Page 20. Section 115.
Sub-section 10.

Line 2. *After* " period " *insert* " and to such extent ".

Line 3. *After* " or carriage " (as inserted by Amendments No. 1, notified in Army Order 40 of 1928) *insert*—

Amdt. 3
June, 1934

or the sale and purchase of horses or carriages of any class or description so specified.

110
General
4587

Line 3. *For* " persons " *substitute* " person ".

Insert new sub-section—

Amdt. 3
June, 1934

(11) The power conferred by this section to issue a requisition of emergency shall include power to issue a requisition of emergency revoking, amending or varying a requisition of emergency previously issued.

110
General
4587

(7930)

6. Pages 21 and 22. *Delete* Form A, Requisition of Emergency, and *substitute—*

Requisition of Emergency. **(A.)**

Amdt. 3
June, 1934

Requisition of Emergency (under the Army Act, Section 115) for the provision of Carriages, Animals and Vessels, and also of Food, Forage and Stores of every description for use of His Majesty's Forces.

110
General
4587

Whereas His Majesty in pursuance of Section 115 of the Army Act has by Order dated...........................

and signified by ....

.........................a Secretary of State, been pleased to order and authorize any General or Field Officer Commanding His Majesty's Regular Forces in any military district or place in Great Britain or Northern Ireland, to issue a requisition of emergency under the said section for the provision for the purposes mentioned in the requisition of such carriages, animals and vessels as are mentioned in the said section, and also of food, forage and stores of every description (*and to order and authorize any such officer to extend such requisition to the provision of carriages, animals, vessels, food, forage and stores for the purpose of being purchased, as well as being hired, on behalf of the Crown*).*

Requisition to be filled in and signed by General or Field Officer authorized to issue it, or under S. 171 of the Army Act by a Staff Officer who is authorized to act on behalf of those Officers, and shall be expressed as signing on their behalf.

Now therefore, I,.....................................being a General (Field) Officer, Commanding His Majesty's Regular Forces in.. do hereby issue a Requisition of Emergency in pursuance of the said Order and do hereby require Justices of the Peace to issue their warrants for the provision of such carriages, animals, vessels, food, forage and stores as aforesaid as the same may be demanded by authorized Officers for the use of His Majesty's Forces in a fit state for such purpose.

And I further authorize....................................... to require that the carriages and horses furnished under such warrant shall be delivered at such place (not being more than (i) 250 miles from the premises of the owner in the case of any mechanically propelled carriage or trailer if being purchased, or (ii) 100 miles in the case of any mechanically propelled carriage or trailer if being hired, or (iii) 10 miles in the case of any other carriage or any horse) and at such times as may be specified by the said.................................

Place.......................   Signature........................

Date ....

---

* The words in brackets will be deleted if a proclamation ordering the Army Reserve to be called out on permanent service is not in force ; such deletion to be initialled.

7. Page 23. Form (B). Heading. *For* " **HORSES, VEHICLES, FOOD, FORAGE, STORES, OF EVERY DESCRIPTION.**" *substitute* **CARRIAGES, ANIMALS AND VESSELS, AND ALSO FOOD, FORAGE AND STORES OF EVERY DESCRIPTION.**

8. Page 89. Form (D). Marginal note. *After* " vehicles," *insert* " vessels,"

By Command of the Army Council,

WAR OFFICE,
30*th June*, 1934

ND - #0528 - 270225 - C0 - 180/122/4 - PB - 9781908487735 - Matt Lamination